YOU WANT IT? THEN GO GET IT!

Printed in the USA by A2Z Books, LLC. Copyright by Lisa Walker-Holloway of JMC Career Solutions & Consulting LLC. All rights reserved. This book or any portion thereof may not be reproduced or used in any manner whatsoever without the express written permission of the publisher except for the use of brief quotations in book review Printed in the United States. First Printing ISBN 978-1-943284-53-5

www.A2ZBookspublishing.net

The journal that offers a **3-D** formula that will help you picture your *dreams* in a way that you can *reach* out, *touch* them and *get* them!

> *The power to believe in what you want to become!*
>
> Lisa Walker-Holloway

> *The big secret in life is that there is no secret. Whatever your goal, you can get there if you are willing to work.*
>
> Oprah Winfrey

THIS JOURNAL BELONGS TO:

_____

_____

_____

Before you get started -THE FORMULA

The *Get It* journal, was designed to help you take your *dreams* to reality.

The journal uses a **3-D** formula to help you picture your *dreams* in a way that you can *reach* out, *touch* them and *get* them.

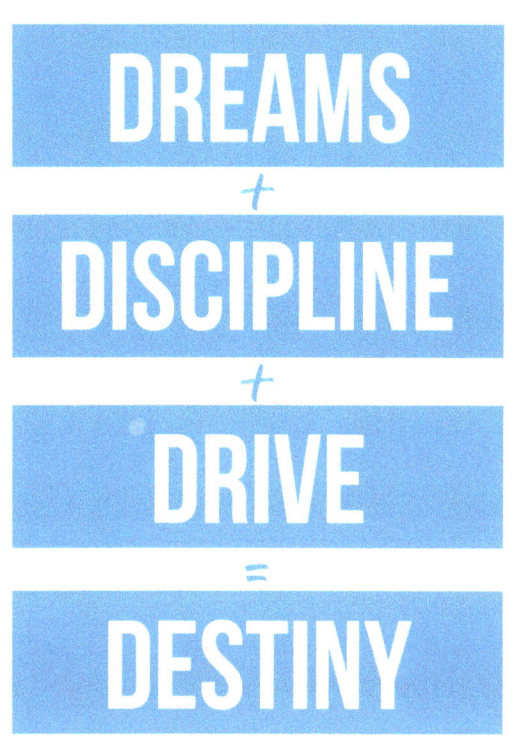

Get closer to your Dreams, with Discipline, and Drive, to reach your Destiny!

The journal will help you:

- Turn your *dreams* into goals.
- Turn your goals into S.M.A.R.T goals.
- Create timelines and deliverables to get you to the next step.
- Chart your progress with weekly, monthly and quarterly check-ins.
- Write down important notes and updates.

Before you get started - GLOSSARY

What's a goal?
A goal is something you intend to accomplish or attain.

What's a S.M.A.R.T goal?
A best practice technique that helps you qualify your goals to ensure they are effective and can actually be achieved.

The acronym SMART stands for:
- Specific
- Measurable
- Attainable
- Realistic
- Time bound

What's a long term goal?
A goal that can be achieved in 12 months or more.

What's a short term goal?
A goal that can be achieved in less than 12 months.

What is a resource?
A source of information, support or expertise.

- **Specific**- Be specific as to what you would like to accomplish.

- **Measurable**- Is your goal measurable? How will you be able to determine how close you are to achieving your goal?

- **Attainable**- Is your goal attainable? Do you have the tools to achieve the goal? Are you setting yourself up for failure?

- **Realistic**- Does your goal make sense? Is your goal realistic? Can you actually achieve the goal you have set for yourself?

- **Time bound**- Have you created a timeline for your goal to be met? It's important to attach a realistic target date to achieve your goals.

- **Accountability Buddy:** A trusted friend that helps you stay the course meeting your goals.

Before you get started
THE "GET IT" PROMISE

As I begin to create my purpose driven life I promise to use all of my power, energy, passion and focus on my new journey. I will commit my time, discipline and drive to make my dreams become my destiny.

Signature:

Date:

> *Whatever the mind can conceive and believe, it can achieve.*
>
> Napoleon Hill

DREAMS

What does your dream look like? Here you can place a picture to remind you of the goal you are trying to accomplish. No picture? Use this area to doodle or draw your vision.

DREAMS

"A series of thoughts, images, or emotions"

Make your dream a goal and make your goal S.M.A.R.T.

Specific - What is your goal? What would you like to accomplish?
_____
_____
_____
_____

Measurable - How will you be able to determine how close you are to achieving your goal?
_____
_____
_____
_____

Attainable - Do you have the tools to achieve the goal?
_____
_____
_____
_____

Realistic - Does your goal make sense?
_____
_____
_____
_____

Time bound - What's your target date to accomplish the goal?
_____
_____
_____
_____

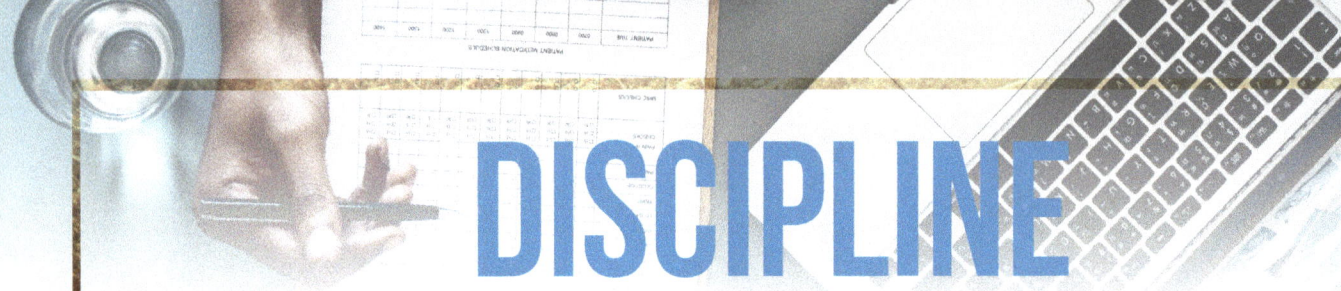

DISCIPLINE

"Train oneself to do something in a controlled and habitual way"

What steps do you need to take to achieve your goal ?

Use this page to create timelines and deliverables to get you to the next step.

Step 1.
_____
_____
_____

Complete by: _____

Step 2.
_____
_____
_____

Complete by: _____

Step 3.
_____
_____
_____

Complete by: _____

Step 4.
_____
_____
_____

Complete by: _____

What resources do you need to help you complete each step?

> *Destiny is no matter of chance.
> It is a matter of choice. It is not a
> thing to be waited for, it is a thing
> to be achieved.*

William Jennings Bryan

MONTH: _____

Use the calendar to chart your daily, weekly, and monthly to do's, reminders, and deadlines!!

SUNDAY	MONDAY	TUESDAY	WEDNESDAY

THURSDAY	FRIDAY	SATURDAY

NOTES

DRIVE

"To strive vigorously toward a goal or objective; to work, play, or try, wholeheartedly and with determination"

What is your "*Why*" and what motivates you to achieve your goals?

_____
_____
_____
_____
_____
_____
_____
_____
_____
_____
_____
_____
_____
_____
_____

"GET IT" ACTION PLAN

The *Get It* Checklist:

☐ Turned my dream into a goal.

☐ Made my goal S.M.A.R.T.

☐ I created timelines and deliverables to get me closer to achieving my goal.

☐ I've shared my goal with my Accountability Buddy and we have scheduled weekly, monthly, and quarterly progress check in's.

My goal is:
_____
_____

My target date to accomplish my goal is:
_____

I will monitor my progress by:
_____
_____

Below are the key steps I need to achieve my goal.

1. _____
2. _____
3. _____

I will use the following resources to help me achieve my goal.

1. _____
2. _____
3. _____

My motivation to accomplish my goal is:
_____
_____

DESTINY

"The things that someone or something will experience in the future"

Now that you have followed the **3-D** formula how does it feel to have achieved your goal?

What does success feel like to you?
_____
_____
_____
_____
_____

What did you learn?
_____
_____
_____
_____
_____

What are your takeaways?
_____
_____
_____
_____
_____
_____

NOTES

DREAMS

What does your dream look like? Here you can place a picture to remind you of the goal you are trying to accomplish. No picture? Use this area to doodle or draw your vision.

DREAMS

"A series of thoughts, images, or emotions"

Make your dream a goal and make your goal S.M.A.R.T.

Specific - What is your goal? What would you like to accomplish?
_____
_____
_____
_____

Measurable - How will you be able to determine how close you are to achieving your goal?
_____
_____
_____

Attainable - Do you have the tools to achieve the goal?
_____
_____
_____
_____

Realistic - Does your goal make sense?
_____
_____
_____
_____

Time bound - What's your target date to accomplish the goal?
_____
_____
_____
_____

DISCIPLINE

"Train oneself to do something in a controlled and habitual way"

What steps do you need to take to achieve your goal ?

Use this page to create timelines and deliverables to get you to the next step.

Step 1.
_____
_____
_____

Complete by: _____

Step 2.
_____
_____
_____

Complete by: _____

Step 3.
_____
_____
_____

Complete by: _____

Step 4.
_____
_____
_____

Complete by: _____

What resources do you need to help you complete each step?

> There's no luck in #business.
> There's only drive, determination,
> and more drive.

Sophie Kinsella

MONTH: _____

Use the calendar to chart your daily, weekly, and monthly to do's, reminders, and deadlines!!

SUNDAY	MONDAY	TUESDAY	WEDNESDAY

THURSDAY	FRIDAY	SATURDAY

NOTES

DRIVE

"To strive vigorously toward a goal or objective; to work, play, or try, wholeheartedly and with determination"

What is your *"Why"* and what motivates you to achieve your goals?

_____
_____
_____
_____
_____
_____
_____
_____
_____
_____
_____
_____
_____
_____
_____
_____

"GET IT" ACTION PLAN

The *Get It* Checklist:

- [ ] Turned my dream into a goal.
- [ ] Made my goal S.M.A.R.T.
- [ ] I created timelines and deliverables to get me closer to achieving my goal.
- [ ] I've shared my goal with my Accountability Buddy and we have scheduled weekly, monthly, and quarterly progress check in's.

My goal is:
_____
_____

My target date to accomplish my goal is:
_____

I will monitor my progress by:
_____
_____

Below are the key steps I need to achieve my goal.

1. _____
2. _____
3. _____

I will use the following resources to help me achieve my goal.

1. _____
2. _____
3. _____

My motivation to accomplish my goal is:
_____
_____

DESTINY

"The things that someone or something will experience in the future"

Now that you have followed the **3-D** formula how does it feel to have achieved your goal?

What does success feel like to you?
_____
_____
_____
_____
_____

What did you learn?
_____
_____
_____
_____
_____

What are your takeaways?
_____
_____
_____
_____
_____

NOTES

DREAMS

What does your dream look like? Here you can place a picture to remind you of the goal you are trying to accomplish. No picture? Use this area to doodle or draw your vision.

DREAMS

"A series of thoughts, images, or emotions"

Make your dream a goal and make your goal S.M.A.R.T.

Specific - What is your goal? What would you like to accomplish?
_____
_____
_____
_____

Measurable - How will you be able to determine how close you are to achieving your goal?
_____
_____
_____
_____

Attainable - Do you have the tools to achieve the goal?
_____
_____
_____
_____

Realistic - Does your goal make sense?
_____
_____
_____
_____

Time bound - What's your target date to accomplish the goal?
_____
_____
_____
_____

> *If you can't fly, then run. If you can't run, then walk. If you can't walk, then crawl. but whatever you do, you have to keep moving forward.*
>
> Martin Luther King Jr

DISCIPLINE

"Train oneself to do something in a controlled and habitual way"

What steps do you need to take to achieve your goal ?

Use this page to create timelines and deliverables to get you to the next step.

Step 1.
_____
_____
_____

Complete by: _____

Step 2.
_____
_____
_____

Complete by: _____

Step 3.
_____
_____
_____

Complete by: _____

Step 4.
_____
_____
_____

Complete by: _____

What resources do you need to help you complete each step?

MONTH: _____

Use the calendar to chart your daily, weekly, and monthly to do's, reminders, and deadlines!!

SUNDAY	MONDAY	TUESDAY	WEDNESDAY

THURSDAY	FRIDAY	SATURDAY

NOTES

_____
_____
_____
_____
_____
_____
_____
_____
_____
_____
_____
_____
_____
_____
_____
_____
_____
_____
_____
_____
_____
_____
_____
_____
_____
_____
_____
_____
_____

> *It was character that got us out of bed, commitment that moved us into action and discipline that enabled us to follow through.*

Zig Ziglar

DRIVE

"To strive vigorously toward a goal or objective; to work, play, or try, wholeheartedly and with determination"

What is your "*Why*" and what motivates you to achieve your goals?

_____
_____
_____
_____
_____
_____
_____
_____
_____
_____
_____
_____
_____
_____

"GET IT" ACTION PLAN

The *Get It* Checklist:

☐ Turned my dream into a goal.

☐ Made my goal S.M.A.R.T.

☐ I created timelines and deliverables to get me closer to achieving my goal.

☐ I've shared my goal with my Accountability Buddy and we have scheduled weekly, monthly, and quarterly progress check in's.

My goal is:
_____
_____

My target date to accomplish my goal is:
_____

I will monitor my progress by:
_____
_____

Below are the key steps I need to achieve my goal.

1. _____
2. _____
3. _____

I will use the following resources to help me achieve my goal.

1. _____
2. _____
3. _____

My motivation to accomplish my goal is:
_____
_____

DESTINY

"The things that someone or something will experience in the future"

Now that you have followed the **3-D** formula how does it feel to have achieved your goal?

What does success feel like to you?
_____
_____
_____
_____
_____

What did you learn?
_____
_____
_____
_____
_____

What are your takeaways?
_____
_____
_____
_____
_____
_____

NOTES

> *The distance between Dreams and reality is called discipline.*
>
> Anonymous

2ND QUARTER GOALS

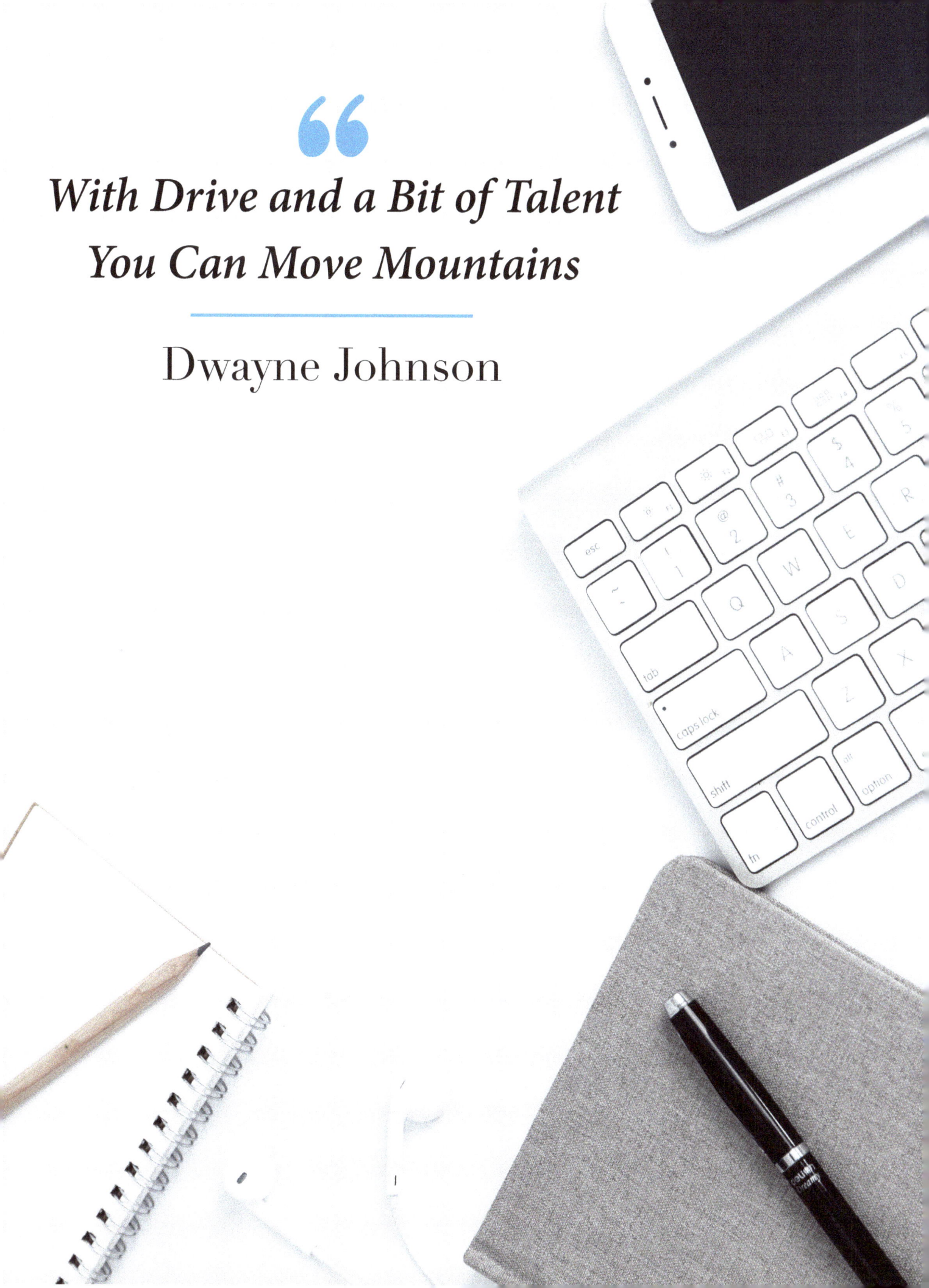

> *With Drive and a Bit of Talent You Can Move Mountains*
>
> Dwayne Johnson

DREAMS

What does your dream look like? Here you can place a picture to remind you of the goal you are trying to accomplish. No picture? Use this area to doodle or draw your vision.

DREAMS

"A series of thoughts, images, or emotions"

Make your dream a goal and make your goal S.M.A.R.T.

Specific - What is your goal? What would you like to accomplish?
_____
_____
_____
_____

Measurable - How will you be able to determine how close you are to achieving your goal?
_____
_____
_____

Attainable - Do you have the tools to achieve the goal?
_____
_____
_____
_____

Realistic - Does your goal make sense?
_____
_____
_____
_____

Time bound - What's your target date to accomplish the goal?
_____
_____
_____
_____

DISCIPLINE

"Train oneself to do something in a controlled and habitual way"

What steps do you need to take to achieve your goal ?

Use this page to create timelines and deliverables to get you to the next step.

Step 1.
_____
_____
_____

Complete by: _____

Step 2.
_____
_____
_____

Complete by: _____

Step 3.
_____
_____
_____

Complete by: _____

Step 4.
_____
_____
_____

Complete by: _____

What resources do you need to help you complete each step?

> The biggest adventure you can take is to live the life of your Dreams.

Oprah Winfrey

MONTH: _____

Use the calendar to chart your daily, weekly, and monthly to do's, reminders, and deadlines!!

SUNDAY	MONDAY	TUESDAY	WEDNESDAY

THURSDAY	FRIDAY	SATURDAY

NOTES

DRIVE

"To strive vigorously toward a goal or objective; to work, play, or try, wholeheartedly and with determination"

What is your *"Why"* and what motivates you to achieve your goals?

_____
_____
_____
_____
_____
_____
_____
_____
_____
_____
_____
_____
_____
_____
_____

> *Dreams are the seeds of change. Nothing ever grows without a seed, and nothing ever changes without a dream.*
>
> Debby Boone

"GET IT" ACTION PLAN

The *Get It* Checklist:

☐ Turned my dream into a goal.

☐ Made my goal S.M.A.R.T.

☐ I created timelines and deliverables to get me closer to achieving my goal.

☐ I've shared my goal with my Accountability Buddy and we have scheduled weekly, monthly, and quarterly progress check in's.

My goal is:
_____
_____

My target date to accomplish my goal is:
_____

I will monitor my progress by:
_____
_____

Below are the key steps I need to achieve my goal.

1. _____
2. _____
3. _____

I will use the following resources to help me achieve my goal.

1. _____
2. _____
3. _____

My motivation to accomplish my goal is:
_____
_____

DESTINY

"The things that someone or something will experience in the future"

Now that you have followed the **3-D** formula how does it feel to have achieved your goal?

What does success feel like to you?
_____
_____
_____
_____
_____

What did you learn?
_____
_____
_____
_____
_____

What are your takeaways?
_____
_____
_____
_____
_____

NOTES

> *Every great dream begins with a dreamer. Always remember, you have within you the strength, the patience, and the passion to reach for the stars to change the world.*
>
> Harriet Tubman

DREAMS

What does your dream look like? Here you can place a picture to remind you of the goal you are trying to accomplish. No picture? Use this area to doodle or draw your vision.

DREAMS

"A series of thoughts, images, or emotions"

Make your dream a goal and make your goal S.M.A.R.T.

Specific - What is your goal? What would you like to accomplish?
_____
_____
_____
_____

Measurable - How will you be able to determine how close you are to achieving your goal?
_____
_____
_____
_____

Attainable - Do you have the tools to achieve the goal?
_____
_____
_____
_____

Realistic - Does your goal make sense?
_____
_____
_____
_____

Time bound - What's your target date to accomplish the goal?
_____
_____
_____
_____

DISCIPLINE

"Train oneself to do something in a controlled and habitual way"

What steps do you need to take to achieve your goal ?

Use this page to create timelines and deliverables to get you to the next step.

Step 1.
_____
_____
_____

Complete by: _____

Step 2.
_____
_____
_____

Complete by: _____

Step 3.
_____
_____
_____

Complete by: _____

Step 4.
_____
_____
_____

Complete by: _____

What resources do you need to help you complete each step?

> ❝
> *A dream doesn't become reality through magic; it takes sweat, determination, and hard work.*
>
> Colin Powell

MONTH: _____

Use the calendar to chart your daily, weekly, and monthly to do's, reminders, and deadlines!!

SUNDAY	MONDAY	TUESDAY	WEDNESDAY

THURSDAY	FRIDAY	SATURDAY

NOTES

DRIVE

"To strive vigorously toward a goal or objective; to work, play, or try, wholeheartedly and with determination"

What is your *"Why"* and what motivates you to achieve your goals?

_____
_____
_____
_____
_____
_____
_____
_____
_____
_____
_____
_____
_____
_____
_____
_____

"GET IT" ACTION PLAN

The *Get It* Checklist:

☐ Turned my dream into a goal.

☐ Made my goal S.M.A.R.T.

☐ I created timelines and deliverables to get me closer to achieving my goal.

☐ I've shared my goal with my Accountability Buddy and we have scheduled weekly, monthly, and quarterly progress check in's.

My goal is:
_____
_____

My target date to accomplish my goal is:
_____

I will monitor my progress by:
_____
_____

Below are the key steps I need to achieve my goal.
1. _____
2. _____
3. _____

I will use the following resources to help me achieve my goal.
1. _____
2. _____
3. _____

My motivation to accomplish my goal is:
_____
_____

DESTINY

"The things that someone or something will experience in the future"

Now that you have followed the **3-D** formula how does it feel to have achieved your goal?

What does success feel like to you?
_____
_____
_____
_____
_____

What did you learn?
_____
_____
_____
_____
_____

What are your takeaways?
_____
_____
_____
_____
_____
_____

NOTES

DREAMS

What does your dream look like? Here you can place a picture to remind you of the goal you are trying to accomplish. No picture? Use this area to doodle or draw your vision.

DREAMS

"A series of thoughts, images, or emotions"

Make your dream a goal and make your goal S.M.A.R.T.

Specific - What is your goal? What would you like to accomplish?
_____
_____
_____
_____

Measurable - How will you be able to determine how close you are to achieving your goal?
_____
_____
_____
_____

Attainable - Do you have the tools to achieve the goal?
_____
_____
_____
_____

Realistic - Does your goal make sense?
_____
_____
_____
_____

Time bound - What's your target date to accomplish the goal?
_____
_____
_____
_____

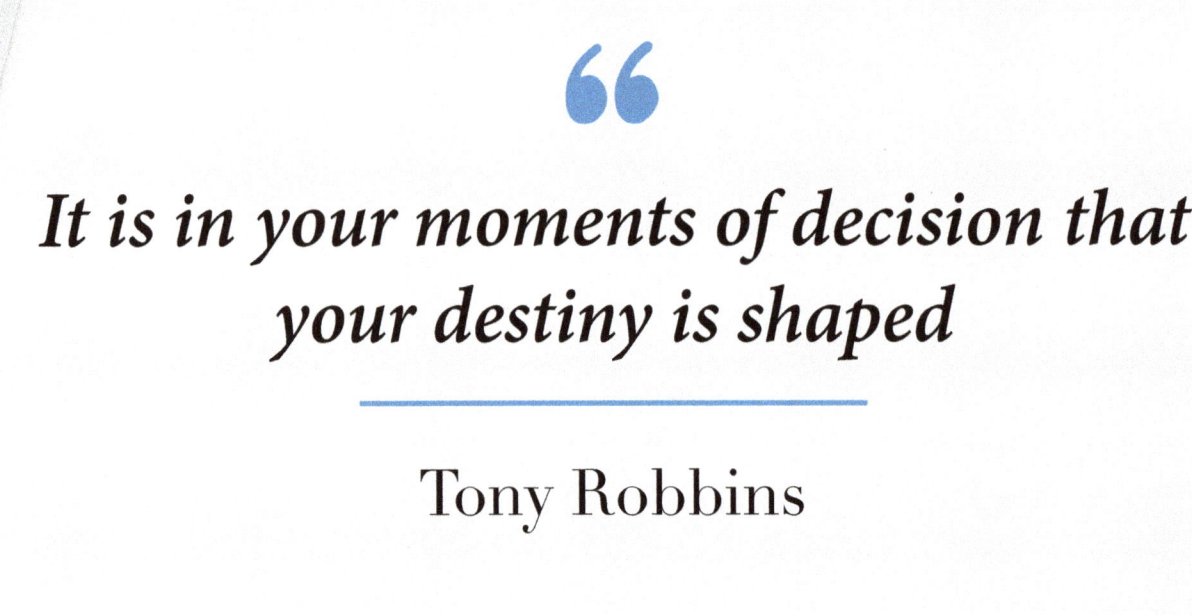

> *It is in your moments of decision that your destiny is shaped*
>
> Tony Robbins

DISCIPLINE

"Train oneself to do something in a controlled and habitual way"

What steps do you need to take to achieve your goal ?

Use this page to create timelines and deliverables to get you to the next step.

Step 1.
_____
_____
_____

Complete by: _____

Step 2.
_____
_____
_____

Complete by: _____

Step 3.
_____
_____
_____

Complete by: _____

Step 4.
_____
_____
_____

Complete by: _____

What resources do you need to help you complete each step?

MONTH: _____

Use the calendar to chart your daily, weekly, and monthly to do's, reminders, and deadlines!!

SUNDAY	MONDAY	TUESDAY	WEDNESDAY

THURSDAY	FRIDAY	SATURDAY

NOTES

> *You miss 100% of the shots you don't take.*
>
> Wayne Gretzky

DRIVE

"To strive vigorously toward a goal or objective; to work, play, or try, wholeheartedly and with determination"

What is your *"Why"* and what motivates you to achieve your goals?

_____
_____
_____
_____
_____
_____
_____
_____
_____
_____
_____
_____
_____
_____

"GET IT" ACTION PLAN

The *Get It* Checklist:

☐ Turned my dream into a goal.

☐ Made my goal S.M.A.R.T.

☐ I created timelines and deliverables to get me closer to achieving my goal.

☐ I've shared my goal with my Accountability Buddy and we have scheduled weekly, monthly, and quarterly progress check in's.

My goal is:
_____
_____

My target date to accomplish my goal is:
_____

I will monitor my progress by:
_____
_____

Below are the key steps I need to achieve my goal.

1. _____
2. _____
3. _____

I will use the following resources to help me achieve my goal.

1. _____
2. _____
3. _____

My motivation to accomplish my goal is:
_____
_____

DESTINY

"The things that someone or something will experience in the future"

Now that you have followed the **3-D** formula how does it feel to have achieved your goal?

What does success feel like to you?
_____
_____
_____
_____
_____

What did you learn?
_____
_____
_____
_____
_____

What are your takeaways?
_____
_____
_____
_____
_____

NOTES

3RD QUARTER GOALS

DREAMS

What does your dream look like? Here you can place a picture to remind you of the goal you are trying to accomplish. No picture? Use this area to doodle or draw your vision.

DREAMS

"A series of thoughts, images, or emotions"

Make your dream a goal and make your goal S.M.A.R.T.

Specific - What is your goal? What would you like to accomplish?
_____
_____
_____
_____

Measurable - How will you be able to determine how close you are to achieving your goal?
_____
_____
_____

Attainable - Do you have the tools to achieve the goal?
_____
_____
_____
_____

Realistic - Does your goal make sense?
_____
_____
_____
_____

Time bound - What's your target date to accomplish the goal?
_____
_____
_____
_____

DISCIPLINE

"Train oneself to do something in a controlled and habitual way"

What steps do you need to take to achieve your goal?

Use this page to create timelines and deliverables to get you to the next step.

Step 1.
_____
_____
_____

Complete by: _____

Step 2.
_____
_____
_____

Complete by: _____

Step 3.
_____
_____
_____

Complete by: _____

Step 4.
_____
_____
_____

Complete by: _____

What resources do you need to help you complete each step?

> ## *The only person you are destined to become is the person you decide to be.*
>
> ---
>
> Ralph Waldo Emerson

MONTH: _____

Use the calendar to chart your daily, weekly, and monthly to do's, reminders, and deadlines!!

SUNDAY	MONDAY	TUESDAY	WEDNESDAY

THURSDAY	FRIDAY	SATURDAY

NOTES

> ❝
> *All our Dreams can come true, if we have the courage to pursue them.*
>
> Walt Disney

DRIVE

"To strive vigorously toward a goal or objective; to work, play, or try, wholeheartedly and with determination"

What is your "*Why*" and what motivates you to achieve your goals?

_____
_____
_____
_____
_____
_____
_____
_____
_____
_____
_____
_____
_____
_____

"GET IT" ACTION PLAN

The *Get It* Checklist:

☐ Turned my dream into a goal.

☐ Made my goal S.M.A.R.T.

☐ I created timelines and deliverables to get me closer to achieving my goal.

☐ I've shared my goal with my Accountability Buddy and we have scheduled weekly, monthly, and quarterly progress check in's.

My goal is:
_____
_____

My target date to accomplish my goal is:
_____

I will monitor my progress by:
_____
_____

Below are the key steps I need to achieve my goal.

1. _____
2. _____
3. _____

I will use the following resources to help me achieve my goal.

1. _____
2. _____
3. _____

My motivation to accomplish my goal is:
_____
_____

DESTINY

"The things that someone or something will experience in the future"

Now that you have followed the **3-D** formula how does it feel to have achieved your goal?

What does success feel like to you?
_____
_____
_____
_____
_____

What did you learn?
_____
_____
_____
_____
_____

What are your takeaways?
_____
_____
_____
_____
_____
_____

NOTES

> **66**
>
> *Believe in yourself. You are braver than you think, more talented than you know, and capable of more than you imagine.*
>
> Roy T. Bennett

DREAMS

What does your dream look like? Here you can place a picture to remind you of the goal you are trying to accomplish. No picture? Use this area to doodle or draw your vision.

DREAMS

"A series of thoughts, images, or emotions"

Make your dream a goal and make your goal S.M.A.R.T.

Specific - What is your goal? What would you like to accomplish?
_____
_____
_____
_____

Measurable - How will you be able to determine how close you are to achieving your goal?
_____
_____
_____
_____

Attainable - Do you have the tools to achieve the goal?
_____
_____
_____
_____

Realistic - Does your goal make sense?
_____
_____
_____
_____

Time bound - What's your target date to accomplish the goal?
_____
_____
_____
_____

DISCIPLINE

"Train oneself to do something in a controlled and habitual way"

What steps do you need to take to achieve your goal ?

Use this page to create timelines and deliverables to get you to the next step.

Step 1.
_____
_____
_____

Complete by: _____

Step 2.
_____
_____
_____

Complete by: _____

Step 3.
_____
_____
_____

Complete by: _____

Step 4.
_____
_____
_____

Complete by: _____

What resources do you need to help you complete each step?

> *I learned that courage was not the absence of fear, but the triumph over it. The brave man is not he who does not feel afraid, but he who conquers that fear.*

Nelson Mandela

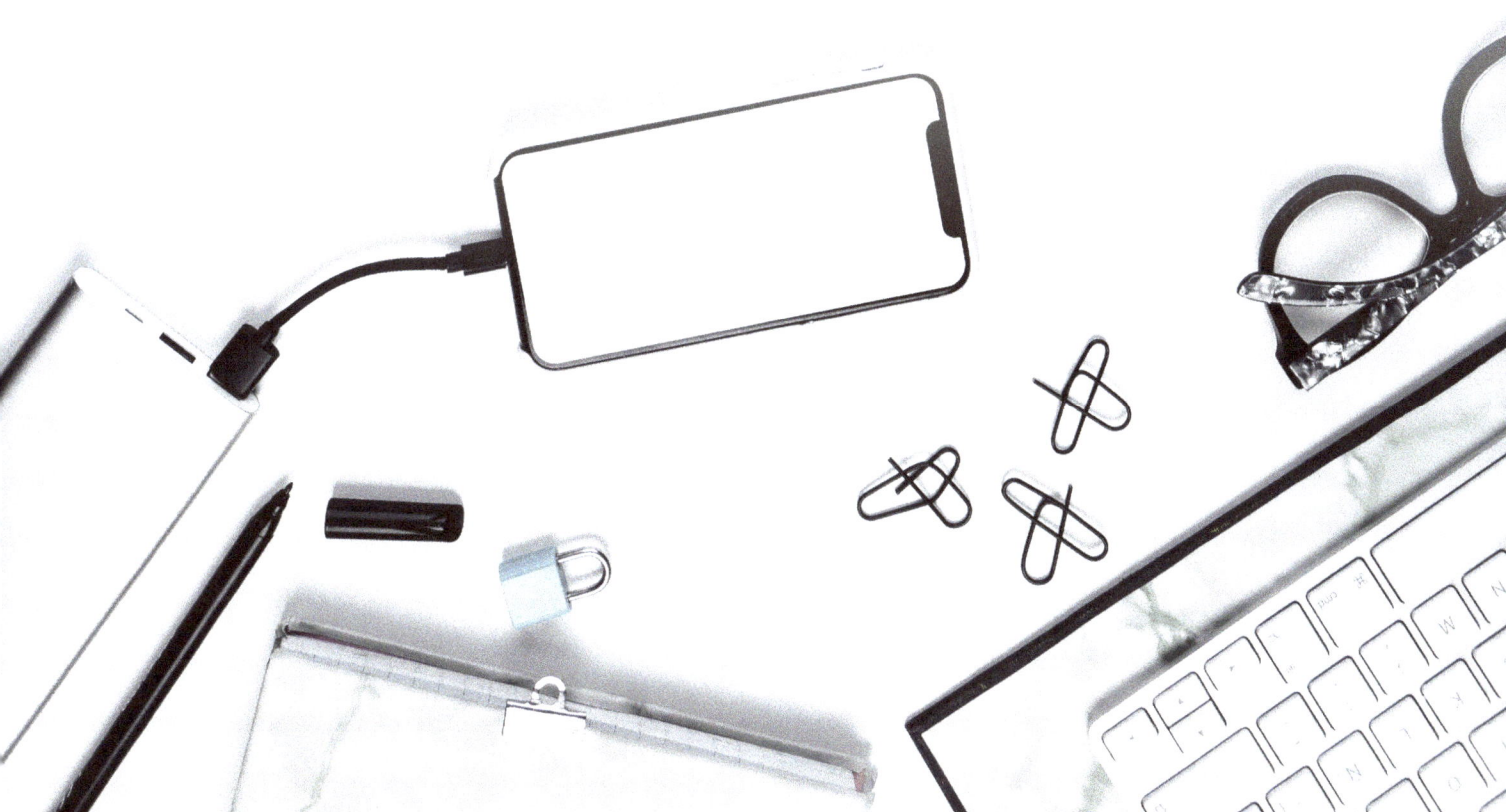

MONTH: _____

Use the calendar to chart your daily, weekly, and monthly to do's, reminders, and deadlines!!

SUNDAY	MONDAY	TUESDAY	WEDNESDAY

THURSDAY	FRIDAY	SATURDAY

NOTES

DRIVE

"To strive vigorously toward a goal or objective; to work, play, or try, wholeheartedly and with determination"

What is your *"Why"* and what motivates you to achieve your goals?

_____
_____
_____
_____
_____
_____
_____
_____
_____
_____
_____
_____
_____
_____
_____

"GET IT" ACTION PLAN

The *Get It* Checklist:

☐ Turned my dream into a goal.

☐ Made my goal S.M.A.R.T.

☐ I created timelines and deliverables to get me closer to achieving my goal.

☐ I've shared my goal with my Accountability Buddy and we have scheduled weekly, monthly, and quarterly progress check in's.

My goal is:
_____
_____

My target date to accomplish my goal is:
_____

I will monitor my progress by:
_____
_____

Below are the key steps I need to achieve my goal.

1. _____
2. _____
3. _____

I will use the following resources to help me achieve my goal.

1. _____
2. _____
3. _____

My motivation to accomplish my goal is:
_____
_____

DESTINY

"The things that someone or something will experience in the future"

Now that you have followed the **3-D** formula how does it feel to have achieved your goal?

What does success feel like to you?
_____
_____
_____
_____
_____

What did you learn?
_____
_____
_____
_____
_____

What are your takeaways?
_____
_____
_____
_____
_____

NOTES

DREAMS

What does your dream look like? Here you can place a picture to remind you of the goal you are trying to accomplish. No picture? Use this area to doodle or draw your vision.

DREAMS

"A series of thoughts, images, or emotions"

Make your dream a goal and make your goal S.M.A.R.T.

Specific - What is your goal? What would you like to accomplish?
_____
_____
_____
_____

Measurable - How will you be able to determine how close you are to achieving your goal?
_____
_____
_____

Attainable - Do you have the tools to achieve the goal?
_____
_____
_____
_____

Realistic - Does your goal make sense?
_____
_____
_____
_____

Time bound - What's your target date to accomplish the goal?
_____
_____
_____
_____

There is only one thing that makes a dream impossible to achieve: the fear of failure.

Paulo Coelho

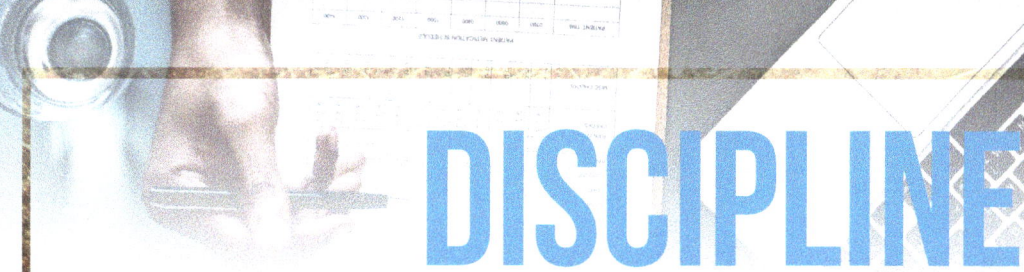

DISCIPLINE

"Train oneself to do something in a controlled and habitual way"

What steps do you need to take to achieve your goal ?

Use this page to create timelines and deliverables to get you to the next step.

Step 1.
_____
_____
_____

Complete by: _____

Step 2.
_____
_____
_____

Complete by: _____

Step 3.
_____
_____
_____

Complete by: _____

Step 4.
_____
_____
_____

Complete by: _____

What resources do you need to help you complete each step?

MONTH: _____

Use the calendar to chart your daily, weekly, and monthly to do's, reminders, and deadlines!!

SUNDAY	MONDAY	TUESDAY	WEDNESDAY

THURSDAY	FRIDAY	SATURDAY

NOTES

> *Your true success in life begins only when you make the commitment to become excellent at what you do.*

— Brian Tracy

DRIVE

"To strive vigorously toward a goal or objective; to work, play, or try, wholeheartedly and with determination"

What is your "*Why*" and what motivates you to achieve your goals?

_____
_____
_____
_____
_____
_____
_____
_____
_____
_____
_____
_____
_____

> **Don't let yesterday take up too much of today.**
>
> Will Rogers

"GET IT" ACTION PLAN

The *Get It* Checklist:

☐ Turned my dream into a goal.

☐ Made my goal S.M.A.R.T.

☐ I created timelines and deliverables to get me closer to achieving my goal.

☐ I've shared my goal with my Accountability Buddy and we have scheduled weekly, monthly, and quarterly progress check in's.

My goal is:
_____
_____

My target date to accomplish my goal is:
_____

I will monitor my progress by:
_____
_____

Below are the key steps I need to achieve my goal.
1. _____
2. _____
3. _____

I will use the following resources to help me achieve my goal.
1. _____
2. _____
3. _____

My motivation to accomplish my goal is:
_____
_____

DESTINY

"The things that someone or something will experience in the future"

Now that you have followed the **3-D** formula how does it feel to have achieved your goal?

What does success feel like to you?
_____
_____
_____
_____
_____

What did you learn?
_____
_____
_____
_____
_____

What are your takeaways?
_____
_____
_____
_____
_____
_____

NOTES

> *Definiteness of purpose is the starting point of all achievement.*

W. Clement Stone

4TH QUARTER GOALS

DREAMS

What does your dream look like? Here you can place a picture to remind you of the goal you are trying to accomplish. No picture? Use this area to doodle or draw your vision.

DREAMS

"A series of thoughts, images, or emotions"

Make your dream a goal and make your goal S.M.A.R.T.

Specific - What is your goal? What would you like to accomplish?
_____
_____
_____
_____

Measurable - How will you be able to determine how close you are to achieving your goal?
_____
_____
_____

Attainable - Do you have the tools to achieve the goal?
_____
_____
_____
_____

Realistic - Does your goal make sense?
_____
_____
_____
_____

Time bound - What's your target date to accomplish the goal?
_____
_____
_____
_____

DISCIPLINE

"Train oneself to do something in a controlled and habitual way"

What steps do you need to take to achieve your goal ?

Use this page to create timelines and deliverables to get you to the next step.

Step 1.
_____
_____
_____

Complete by: _____

Step 2.
_____
_____
_____

Complete by: _____

Step 3.
_____
_____
_____

Complete by: _____

Step 4.
_____
_____
_____

Complete by: _____

What resources do you need to help you complete each step?

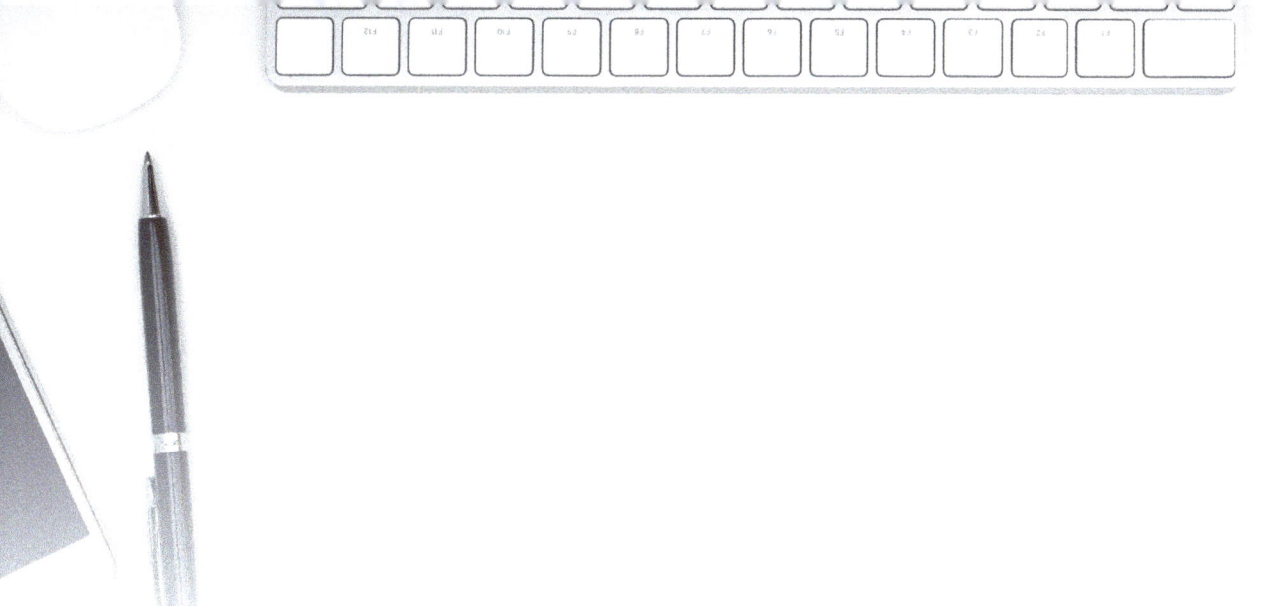

> *If you set goals and go after them with all the determination you can muster, your gifts will take you places that will amaze you.*

Les Brown

MONTH: _____

Use the calendar to chart your daily, weekly, and monthly to do's, reminders, and deadlines!!

SUNDAY	MONDAY	TUESDAY	WEDNESDAY

THURSDAY	FRIDAY	SATURDAY

NOTES

DRIVE

"To strive vigorously toward a goal or objective; to work, play, or try, wholeheartedly and with determination"

What is your "*Why*" and what motivates you to achieve your goals?

"GET IT" ACTION PLAN

The *Get It* Checklist:

☐ Turned my dream into a goal.

☐ Made my goal S.M.A.R.T.

☐ I created timelines and deliverables to get me closer to achieving my goal.

☐ I've shared my goal with my Accountability Buddy and we have scheduled weekly, monthly, and quarterly progress check in's.

My goal is:
_____
_____

My target date to accomplish my goal is:
_____

I will monitor my progress by:
_____
_____

Below are the key steps I need to achieve my goal.
1. _____
2. _____
3. _____

I will use the following resources to help me achieve my goal.
1. _____
2. _____
3. _____

My motivation to accomplish my goal is:
_____
_____

DESTINY

"The things that someone or something will experience in the future"

Now that you have followed the **3-D** formula how does it feel to have achieved your goal?

What does success feel like to you?
_____
_____
_____
_____
_____

What did you learn?
_____
_____
_____
_____
_____

What are your takeaways?
_____
_____
_____
_____
_____

NOTES

DREAMS

What does your dream look like? Here you can place a picture to remind you of the goal you are trying to accomplish. No picture? Use this area to doodle or draw your vision.

DREAMS

"A series of thoughts, images, or emotions"

Make your dream a goal and make your goal S.M.A.R.T.

Specific - What is your goal? What would you like to accomplish?
_____
_____
_____
_____

Measurable - How will you be able to determine how close you are to achieving your goal?
_____
_____
_____
_____

Attainable - Do you have the tools to achieve the goal?
_____
_____
_____
_____

Realistic - Does your goal make sense?
_____
_____
_____
_____

Time bound - What's your target date to accomplish the goal?
_____
_____
_____
_____

If you believe it will work out, you'll see opportunities. If you believe it won't, you will see obstacles.

Wayne Dyer

DISCIPLINE

"Train oneself to do something in a controlled and habitual way"

What steps do you need to take to achieve your goal?

Use this page to create timelines and deliverables to get you to the next step.

Step 1.
_____
_____
_____

Complete by: _____

What resources do you need to help you complete each step?

Step 2.
_____
_____
_____

Complete by: _____

Step 3.
_____
_____
_____

Complete by: _____

Step 4.
_____
_____
_____

Complete by: _____

MONTH: _____

Use the calendar to chart your daily, weekly, and monthly to do's, reminders, and deadlines!!

SUNDAY	MONDAY	TUESDAY	WEDNESDAY

THURSDAY	FRIDAY	SATURDAY

NOTES

Whatever you hold in your mind on a consistent basis is exactly what you will experience in your life.

Tony Robbins

DRIVE

"To strive vigorously toward a goal or objective; to work, play, or try, wholeheartedly and with determination"

What is your "*Why*" and what motivates you to achieve your goals?

_____
_____
_____
_____
_____
_____
_____
_____
_____
_____
_____
_____
_____
_____

"GET IT" ACTION PLAN

The *Get It* Checklist:

☐ Turned my dream into a goal.

☐ Made my goal S.M.A.R.T.

☐ I created timelines and deliverables to get me closer to achieving my goal.

☐ I've shared my goal with my Accountability Buddy and we have scheduled weekly, monthly, and quarterly progress check in's.

My goal is:
_____
_____

My target date to accomplish my goal is:
_____

I will monitor my progress by:
_____
_____

Below are the key steps I need to achieve my goal.

1. _____
2. _____
3. _____

I will use the following resources to help me achieve my goal.

1. _____
2. _____
3. _____

My motivation to accomplish my goal is:
_____
_____

DESTINY

"The things that someone or something will experience in the future"

Now that you have followed the **3-D** formula how does it feel to have achieved your goal?

What does success feel like to you?
_____
_____
_____
_____
_____

What did you learn?
_____
_____
_____
_____
_____

What are your takeaways?
_____
_____
_____
_____
_____

NOTES

> **Strength does not come from physical capacity. It comes from an indomitable will.**

Mahatma Gandhi

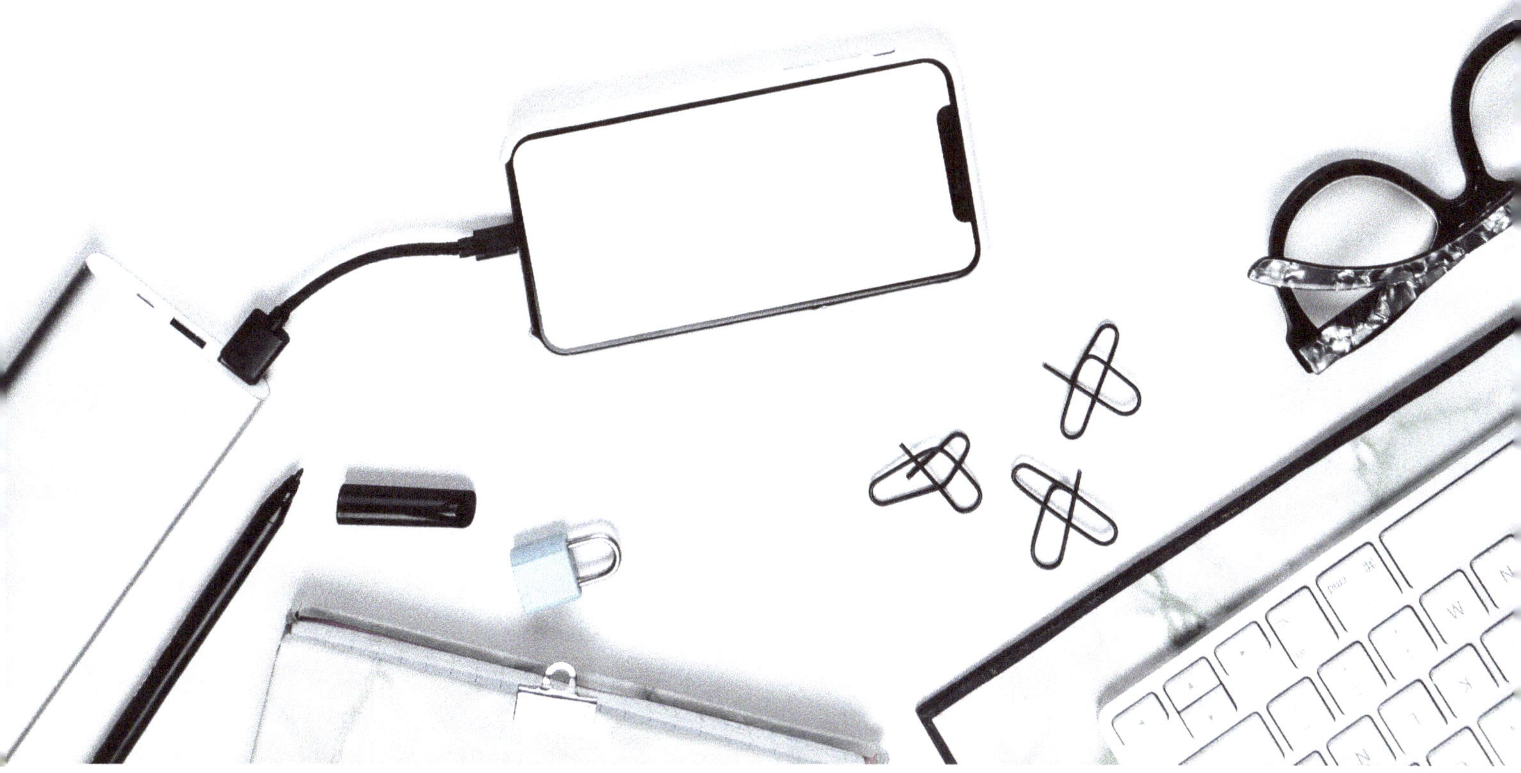

DREAMS

What does your dream look like? Here you can place a picture to remind you of the goal you are trying to accomplish. No picture? Use this area to doodle or draw your vision.

DREAMS

"A series of thoughts, images, or emotions"

Make your dream a goal and make your goal S.M.A.R.T.

Specific - What is your goal? What would you like to accomplish?
_____
_____
_____
_____

Measurable - How will you be able to determine how close you are to achieving your goal?
_____
_____
_____

Attainable - Do you have the tools to achieve the goal?
_____
_____
_____
_____

Realistic - Does your goal make sense?
_____
_____
_____
_____

Time bound - What's your target date to accomplish the goal?
_____
_____
_____
_____

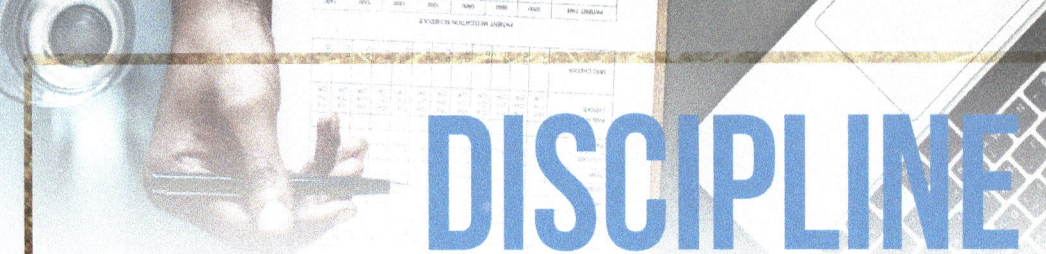

DISCIPLINE

"Train oneself to do something in a controlled and habitual way"

What steps do you need to take to achieve your goal ?

Use this page to create timelines and deliverables to get you to the next step.

Step 1.
_____
_____
_____

Complete by: _____

Step 2.
_____
_____
_____

Complete by: _____

Step 3.
_____
_____
_____

Complete by: _____

Step 4.
_____
_____
_____

Complete by: _____

What resources do you need to help you complete each step?

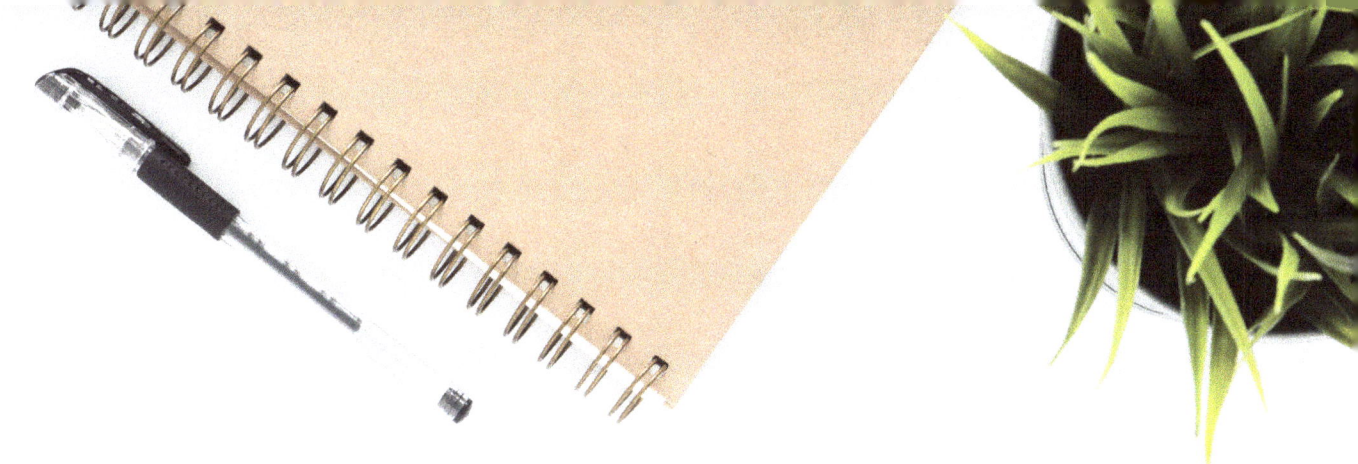

The future belongs to those who believe in the beauty of their Dreams.

Eleanor Roosevelt

MONTH: _____

Use the calendar to chart your daily, weekly, and monthly to do's, reminders, and deadlines!!

SUNDAY	MONDAY	TUESDAY	WEDNESDAY

THURSDAY	FRIDAY	SATURDAY

NOTES

_____
_____
_____
_____
_____
_____
_____
_____
_____
_____
_____
_____
_____
_____
_____
_____
_____
_____
_____
_____
_____
_____
_____
_____
_____
_____
_____

> **Start by doing what's necessary; then do what's possible; and suddenly you are doing the impossible.**
>
> Francis of Assisi

DRIVE

"To strive vigorously toward a goal or objective; to work, play, or try, wholeheartedly and with determination"

What is your "*Why*" and what motivates you to achieve your goals?

_____
_____
_____
_____
_____
_____
_____
_____
_____
_____
_____
_____
_____
_____

"GET IT" ACTION PLAN

The *Get It* Checklist:

☐ Turned my dream into a goal.

☐ Made my goal S.M.A.R.T.

☐ I created timelines and deliverables to get me closer to achieving my goal.

☐ I've shared my goal with my Accountability Buddy and we have scheduled weekly, monthly, and quarterly progress check in's.

My goal is:
_____
_____

My target date to accomplish my goal is:
_____

I will monitor my progress by:
_____
_____

Below are the key steps I need to achieve my goal.
1. _____
2. _____
3. _____

I will use the following resources to help me achieve my goal.
1. _____
2. _____
3. _____

My motivation to accomplish my goal is:
_____
_____

DESTINY

"The things that someone or something will experience in the future"

Now that you have followed the **3-D** formula how does it feel to have achieved your goal?

What does success feel like to you?
_____
_____
_____
_____
_____

What did you learn?
_____
_____
_____
_____
_____

What are your takeaways?
_____
_____
_____
_____
_____
_____

NOTES

We hope that the Get It Journal helped you reach your destiny!

For more information or more resources please visit our website

www.getitjournal.com

Interested in Writing and/or Publishing a book? Visit www.A2ZBookspublishing.net

www.ingramcontent.com/pod-product-compliance
Lightning Source LLC
Chambersburg PA
CBHW051333110526
44591CB00026B/2990